Decarbonizing the Future:

A Comprehensive Guide to Net-Zero

Carbon Concepts

Chapter 1: Introduction to Net-Zero Carbon Concepts

Understanding the Importance of Achieving Net-Zero Carbon

In today's world, the concept of achieving net-zero carbon emissions has become increasingly crucial in the fight against climate change. Net-zero carbon refers to the balance between the amount of greenhouse gases emitted into the atmosphere and the amount removed from it. It is imperative for institutions in all fields and interested individuals from every specialty to understand the importance of achieving net-zero carbon in order to mitigate the impacts of climate change.

One key area was achieving net-zero carbon is essential is transportation. The transportation sector is a significant contributor to greenhouse gas emissions, primarily through the burning of fossil fuels in vehicles. By transitioning to electric vehicles, investing in public transportation, and promoting active modes of transportation such as walking and cycling, we can reduce emissions and move towards net-zero carbon in transportation.

Another critical sector that must focus on achieving net-zero carbon is agriculture. Agriculture is a major source of greenhouse gas emissions, particularly methane and nitrous oxide from livestock and fertilizer use. By implementing sustainable farming practices, reducing food waste, and transitioning to plant-based diets, we can significantly decrease emissions and work towards net-zero carbon in agriculture.

Similarly, the construction industry plays a vital role in achieving net-zero carbon. Buildings account for a significant portion of global emissions, mainly from energy consumption for heating, cooling, and lighting. By designing and constructing energy-efficient buildings, using sustainable materials, and incorporating renewable energy sources, we can reduce emissions and strive towards net-zero carbon in construction.

In conclusion, achieving net-zero carbon is a multifaceted and collaborative effort that requires action across various sectors. By understanding the importance of reducing emissions and transitioning to sustainable practices in transportation, agriculture, construction, energy production, waste management, urban planning, manufacturing, forestry, land use, water management, and consumer goods and services, institutions and individuals can play a significant role in combating climate change and creating a more sustainable future for all.

Overview of the Net-Zero Carbon Concept

The concept of achieving net-zero carbon emissions has gained significant attention in recent years as the global community grapples with the urgent need to address climate change. Net-zero carbon refers to the balance between the amount of carbon dioxide emitted and the amount removed from the atmosphere. This balance is achieved by reducing emissions as much as possible and offsetting any remaining emissions through carbon removal technologies or natural processes.

In transportation, achieving net-zero carbon emissions involves transitioning to electric vehicles, improving fuel efficiency, and investing in public transportation and cycling infrastructure. The transportation sector is a significant contributor to greenhouse gas emissions, making it a key focus area for decarbonization efforts. By shifting towards cleaner modes of transportation and reducing reliance on fossil fuels, we can make significant progress towards achieving net-zero carbon emissions in this sector.

In agriculture, net-zero carbon practices include regenerative farming techniques, soil carbon sequestration, and reducing methane emissions from livestock. Agriculture is a major source of greenhouse gas emissions, particularly methane and nitrous oxide. By implementing sustainable farming practices and investing in agricultural innovation, we can minimize the carbon footprint of food production and contribute to a more sustainable future.

In construction, net-zero carbon initiatives focus on energy-efficient building design, renewable energy integration, and sustainable materials sourcing. The construction industry is a major consumer of energy and resources, making it a key player in the transition to a low-carbon economy. By prioritizing energy efficiency and incorporating renewable technologies into building design, we can reduce emissions associated with construction and operation of buildings.

In energy production, achieving net-zero carbon emissions involves phasing out fossil fuels, increasing renewable energy capacity, and improving energy storage technologies. The energy sector is a major contributor to greenhouse gas emissions, making it a critical focus area for decarbonization efforts. By transitioning to cleaner sources of energy and investing in innovative technologies, we can accelerate the shift towards a net-zero carbon future.

Benefits of Transitioning to a Net-Zero Carbon Future

Transitioning to a net-zero carbon future offers a multitude of benefits across various sectors, making it a crucial step towards achieving environmental sustainability and combating climate change. Institutions in all fields and interested individuals from every specialty stand to gain from embracing the net-zero carbon concept and working towards its realization. By understanding the principles and strategies involved in decarbonizing our future, we can pave the way for a cleaner, healthier planet for current and future generations.

In the realm of transportation, transitioning to a net-zero carbon future involves shifting towards electric vehicles, investing in public transportation systems, and promoting active modes of transport such as cycling and walking. By reducing reliance on fossil fuels and embracing sustainable alternatives, we can significantly lower greenhouse gas emissions and improve air quality in our cities. This not only benefits the environment but also enhances public health and reduces our dependence on finite resources.

In agriculture, adopting net-zero carbon practices such as regenerative farming and agroforestry can help sequester carbon in the soil, mitigate emissions from livestock, and reduce the use of synthetic fertilizers and pesticides. By promoting sustainable agricultural practices, we can not only combat climate change but also enhance biodiversity, improve soil health, and ensure food security for future generations. Investing in research and innovation in sustainable agriculture is key to achieving a net-zero carbon future in this sector.

The construction industry plays a significant role in achieving a net-zero carbon future by implementing energy-efficient building designs, utilizing sustainable materials, and incorporating renewable energy sources. By constructing green buildings and promoting sustainable construction practices, we can reduce the carbon footprint of the built environment and create healthier, more resilient communities. Embracing net-zero carbon principles in construction not only benefits the environment but also lowers operating costs, improves occupant comfort, and enhances the overall quality of life.

In energy production, transitioning to a net-zero carbon future involves phasing out fossil fuel-based power generation in favor of renewable energy sources such as solar, wind, and hydroelectric power. By investing in clean energy technologies and grid modernization, we can decarbonize our electricity supply, reduce emissions, and create a more sustainable energy system. Embracing net-zero carbon practices in energy production not only helps combat climate change but also creates new job opportunities, drives economic growth, and enhances energy security.

Chapter 2: Net-Zero Carbon in Transportation

The Role of Transportation in Carbon Emissions

Transportation plays a crucial role in contributing to carbon emissions, making it a key focus area in achieving net-zero carbon goals. The transportation sector is responsible for a significant portion of global greenhouse gas emissions, primarily through the burning of fossil fuels in vehicles. As institutions in all fields and interested individuals from every specialty, it is essential to understand the impact of transportation on carbon emissions and the steps that can be taken to reduce its environmental footprint.

Net-zero carbon in transportation involves transitioning to cleaner, more sustainable modes of transportation, such as electric vehicles, public transportation, biking, and walking. By shifting away from fossil fuel-powered vehicles to electric vehicles powered by renewable energy sources, we can significantly reduce carbon emissions in the transportation sector. Institutions and individuals can also support the development of infrastructure for electric vehicles, such as charging stations, and promote the use of public transportation to reduce the number of single-occupancy vehicles on the road.

In addition to transitioning to cleaner modes of transportation, reducing the overall demand for transportation can also help in achieving net-zero carbon goals. This can be done through strategies such as telecommuting, carpooling, and promoting mixed-use development that reduces the need for long commutes. By adopting these practices, institutions and individuals can decrease the overall carbon footprint of transportation and contribute to a more sustainable future.

Furthermore, advancements in technology, such as autonomous vehicles and vehicle-to-grid systems, can also play a significant role in reducing carbon emissions in the transportation sector. These technologies have the potential to improve the efficiency of transportation systems, reduce congestion, and optimize energy use, ultimately leading to lower carbon emissions. By investing in and supporting these technologies, institutions and individuals can accelerate the transition to net-zero carbon transportation.

In conclusion, addressing the role of transportation in carbon emissions is essential in achieving net-zero carbon goals. By transitioning to cleaner modes of transportation, reducing overall demand, and embracing technological advancements, institutions in all fields and interested individuals from every specialty can play a critical role in reducing carbon emissions in the transportation sector and creating a more sustainable future for all.

Strategies for Achieving Net-Zero Carbon in Transportation

In order to achieve net-zero carbon in transportation, institutions and individuals must implement a combination of strategies that prioritize reducing emissions and promoting sustainable practices. One key strategy is to transition to electric vehicles (EVs) and invest in renewable energy sources to power them. By electrifying transportation, we can significantly reduce greenhouse gas emissions and move towards a more sustainable future.

Another important strategy for achieving net-zero carbon in transportation is to promote alternative modes of transportation such as walking, biking, and public transit. Encouraging the use of these modes can help reduce the number of vehicles on the road and decrease emissions. Additionally, implementing policies that incentivize carpooling and telecommuting can further reduce the carbon footprint of transportation.

Furthermore, institutions can work towards achieving net-zero carbon in transportation by investing in infrastructure that supports sustainable transportation options. This includes building bike lanes, sidewalks, and public transit systems that are easily accessible and convenient for users. By creating a transportation network that prioritizes sustainability, we can reduce our reliance on fossil fuels and move towards a more environmentally friendly transportation system.

In addition to electrifying transportation and promoting alternative modes of transportation, institutions can also work towards achieving net-zero carbon by implementing policies that reduce the overall demand for transportation. This can be done through land use planning that promotes mixed-use development, reduces urban sprawl, and encourages walking and biking. By creating communities that are more walkable and bikeable, we can reduce the need for long commutes and decrease emissions from transportation.

Overall, achieving net-zero carbon in transportation will require a multi-faceted approach that incorporates a combination of strategies. By transitioning to electric vehicles, promoting alternative modes of transportation, investing in sustainable infrastructure, and reducing the overall demand for transportation, institutions can work towards a more sustainable and environmentally friendly transportation system. It is imperative that institutions in all fields and interested individuals from every specialty come together to implement these strategies and work towards a future free of carbon emissions in transportation.

Case Studies of Successful Net-Zero Carbon Transportation Initiatives

In recent years, there has been a growing focus on achieving net-zero carbon emissions in transportation, as it is one of the largest contributors to greenhouse gas emissions globally. Many institutions and organizations have taken innovative steps to reduce their carbon footprint in this sector. In this subchapter, we will explore some case studies of successful net-zero carbon transportation initiatives that have been implemented around the world.

One notable example is the city of Oslo, Norway, which has set ambitious targets to become a carbon-neutral city by 2030. One of the key initiatives that Oslo has implemented is the promotion of electric vehicles (EVs) through financial incentives and infrastructure development. This has led to a significant increase in the number of EVs on the road, reducing emissions from traditional internal combustion engine vehicles.

Another inspiring case study comes from the logistics industry, where companies like UPS and DHL have invested heavily in alternative fuels and electric delivery vehicles. By transitioning their fleets to cleaner energy sources, these companies have been able to drastically reduce their carbon emissions while still meeting the demands of their customers. This demonstrates that even large-scale transportation operations can make significant progress towards achieving net-zero carbon emissions.

In the aviation sector, airlines like Qantas and United Airlines have been exploring the use of sustainable aviation fuels (SAFs) to reduce their carbon footprint. SAFs are produced from renewable sources such as plant-based oils and waste materials, offering a more sustainable alternative to traditional jet fuels. By incorporating SAFs into their operations, these airlines have been able to lower their overall carbon emissions and contribute to a more sustainable future for air travel.

In the shipping industry, Maersk, the world's largest container shipping company, has committed to achieving net-zero carbon emissions by 2050. To reach this goal, Maersk is investing in new fuel-efficient vessels, exploring alternative fuels like biofuels and hydrogen, and implementing energy-saving technologies. By taking a holistic approach to decarbonization, Maersk is setting a positive example for the maritime sector and demonstrating that net-zero carbon transportation is indeed achievable.

These case studies highlight the diverse range of strategies and technologies that can be employed to achieve net-zero carbon emissions in transportation. By learning from these successful initiatives and implementing similar measures in their own operations, institutions in all fields can play a crucial role in driving the transition towards a more sustainable and decarbonized future.

Chapter 3: Net-Zero Carbon in Agriculture

Impact of Agriculture on Carbon Emissions

As the world continues to grapple with the effects of climate change, the role of agriculture in contributing to carbon emissions cannot be understated. Agriculture is a significant source of greenhouse gas emissions, primarily due to the production and use of fertilizers, livestock, and the conversion of forests to agricultural land. These emissions have a direct impact on the environment, contributing to global warming and climate change. In order to achieve net-zero carbon emissions, it is crucial for institutions in all fields and interested people from every specialty to understand and address the impact of agriculture on carbon emissions.

One of the keyways in which agriculture contributes to carbon emissions is through the production and use of fertilizers. The use of synthetic fertilizers releases nitrous oxide, a potent greenhouse gas, into the atmosphere. Additionally, the production of fertilizers requires energy, which often comes from fossil fuels, further adding to carbon emissions. In order to reduce the carbon footprint of agriculture, it is important to explore sustainable farming practices that minimize the use of synthetic fertilizers and promote organic farming methods.

Livestock farming is another major contributor to carbon emissions in agriculture. Livestock, particularly cows, release methane during digestion, which is a potent greenhouse gas. In addition, the production of livestock feed and the clearing of land for pasture also contribute to carbon emissions. To reduce the impact of livestock farming on carbon emissions, institutions and individuals can explore plant-based alternatives, promote sustainable grazing practices, and invest in livestock feed that is produced using sustainable methods.

The conversion of forests to agricultural land is another significant contributor to carbon emissions in agriculture. Deforestation releases carbon stored in trees into the atmosphere, contributing to global warming. In addition, the clearing of land for agriculture often involves the use of heavy machinery and the burning of vegetation, both of which release carbon dioxide into the air. To address this issue, institutions and individuals can support reforestation efforts, promote sustainable land use practices, and invest in agroforestry initiatives that integrate trees into agricultural landscapes.

In conclusion, the impact of agriculture on carbon emissions is significant and cannot be ignored in the quest for achieving net-zero carbon emissions. By understanding the sources of carbon emissions in agriculture and implementing sustainable practices, institutions in all fields and interested people from every specialty can play a crucial role in reducing the carbon footprint of the agriculture sector. Through collective action and a commitment to sustainability, we can work towards a future where agriculture is no longer a major contributor to carbon emissions, but instead plays a key role in mitigating climate change.

Sustainable Practices for Achieving Net-Zero Carbon in Agriculture

In recent years, there has been an increasing focus on achieving net-zero carbon emissions across various sectors, including agriculture. Sustainable practices play a crucial role in reducing the carbon footprint of the agriculture industry and ultimately contributing to the global goal of achieving net-zero carbon. By implementing sustainable practices, institutions in the agricultural sector can significantly reduce their greenhouse gas emissions and mitigate the impact of climate change.

One key sustainable practice for achieving net-zero carbon in agriculture is the adoption of regenerative farming techniques. Regenerative farming focuses on improving soil health, increasing biodiversity, and sequestering carbon in the soil. By implementing regenerative farming practices such as cover cropping, crop rotation, and reduced tillage, institutions in the agricultural sector can enhance the resilience of their operations while also reducing their carbon emissions.

Another important sustainable practice for achieving net-zero carbon in agriculture is the integration of renewable energy sources. By transitioning to renewable energy sources such as solar, wind, and bioenergy, institutions in the agricultural sector can reduce their reliance on fossil fuels and lower their carbon footprint. Investing in renewable energy technologies not only helps to reduce emissions but also provides long-term cost savings and energy security for agricultural operations.

Additionally, institutions in the agriculture sector can reduce their carbon emissions by optimizing resource use and minimizing waste. By implementing efficient irrigation systems, reducing food waste, and recycling organic matter, agricultural operations can lower their overall carbon footprint. Sustainable practices such as composting, water conservation, and energy efficiency measures can help institutions in the agricultural sector achieve net-zero carbon emissions while also promoting environmental stewardship.

In conclusion, achieving net-zero carbon in agriculture requires a holistic approach that integrates sustainable practices across all aspects of agricultural operations. By adopting regenerative farming techniques, transitioning to renewable energy sources, and optimizing resource use, institutions in the agricultural sector can significantly reduce their carbon emissions and contribute to a more sustainable future. It is essential for institutions in all fields to prioritize sustainable practices in agriculture to mitigate the impacts of climate change and work towards a net-zero carbon future.

Implementing Net-Zero Carbon Agriculture on a Global Scale

Implementing net-zero carbon agriculture on a global scale is a critical component in the transition towards a sustainable future. Agriculture is a significant contributor to greenhouse gas emissions, with practices such as deforestation, intensive farming, and the use of synthetic fertilizers all playing a role in climate change. It is imperative that institutions in all fields and interested individuals from every specialty understand the importance of implementing strategies to reduce carbon emissions in the agricultural sector.

One key strategy for achieving net-zero carbon agriculture is the adoption of regenerative farming practices. These practices focus on building soil health, increasing biodiversity, and sequestering carbon in the soil. By implementing regenerative agriculture techniques such as cover cropping, crop rotation, and reduced tillage, farmers can not only reduce their carbon footprint but also improve the resilience of their land to climate change.

In addition to regenerative farming practices, the widespread adoption of renewable energy sources in agriculture is essential for achieving net-zero carbon emissions. Switching to solar, wind, and other renewable energy sources can help reduce the carbon footprint of farming operations, while also reducing dependence on fossil fuels. Furthermore, the use of energy-efficient technologies and practices, such as precision agriculture and drip irrigation, can further reduce emissions in the agricultural sector.

Collaboration between farmers, policymakers, researchers, and industry stakeholders is crucial for the successful implementation of net-zero carbon agriculture on a global scale. By working together to develop and promote sustainable farming practices, as well as providing support and incentives for farmers to transition to low-carbon technologies, we can accelerate the transition towards a more sustainable agricultural system.

In conclusion, achieving net-zero carbon agriculture is a complex but achievable goal that requires a coordinated effort from all sectors of society. By prioritizing regenerative farming practices, transitioning to renewable energy sources, and fostering collaboration between stakeholders, we can create a more sustainable future for agriculture and mitigate the impacts of climate change. It is imperative that institutions in all fields and interested individuals from every specialty understand the importance of implementing strategies to reduce carbon emissions in the agricultural sector.

Chapter 4: Net-Zero Carbon in Construction

Carbon Footprint of the Construction Industry

The construction industry is a significant contributor to carbon emissions, with buildings and infrastructure accounting for a large portion of global greenhouse gas emissions. As institutions in all fields and interested individuals from every specialty seek to understand and implement net-zero carbon concepts, it is crucial to consider the carbon footprint of the construction industry. By addressing the environmental impact of construction activities, we can move closer to achieving our goal of a sustainable, net-zero carbon future.

One key aspect of reducing the carbon footprint of the construction industry is through the use of sustainable building materials and practices. By incorporating materials with lower embodied carbon, such as recycled or reclaimed materials, and utilizing energy-efficient construction techniques, we can significantly reduce the emissions associated with building construction and operation. Additionally, implementing renewable energy sources, such as solar panels or geothermal heating systems, can further decrease the carbon footprint of buildings and infrastructure.

Furthermore, the construction industry can also focus on reducing waste and improving waste management practices to minimize its environmental impact. By implementing recycling and waste reduction strategies on construction sites, we can divert materials from landfills and reduce the carbon emissions associated with waste disposal. Additionally, using sustainable building practices, such as modular construction or prefabrication, can help to minimize waste and lower the overall carbon footprint of construction projects.

In order to achieve net-zero carbon in the construction industry, it is essential for institutions and individuals to prioritize energy efficiency, sustainable materials, and waste reduction throughout the construction process. By considering the full lifecycle of buildings and infrastructure, from design and construction to operation and maintenance, we can create a more sustainable built environment and reduce the overall carbon emissions of the construction industry. Through collaboration and innovation, we can work towards a net-zero carbon future in the construction sector and contribute to a more sustainable and environmentally friendly world.

In conclusion, addressing the carbon footprint of the construction industry is a crucial step towards achieving our goal of a net-zero carbon future. By implementing sustainable building practices, reducing waste, and prioritizing energy efficiency, we can significantly reduce the environmental impact of construction activities. As institutions in all fields and interested individuals from every specialty strive to decarbonize the future, it is imperative that we prioritize sustainability in the construction industry and work towards a more sustainable built environment for future generations.

Green Building Design and Construction Techniques

Green building design and construction techniques are essential components of achieving the net-zero carbon concept. By incorporating sustainable practices into the building process, institutions can significantly reduce their carbon footprint and contribute to a more environmentally friendly future. These techniques focus on minimizing energy consumption, reducing waste, and utilizing renewable resources to create buildings that are not only efficient but also environmentally responsible.

One key aspect of green building design is the use of energy-efficient materials and technologies. This includes incorporating insulation, high-performance windows and efficient HVAC systems to reduce the energy needed for heating, cooling, and lighting. By using renewable energy sources such as solar panels or wind turbines, buildings can generate their own clean energy and reduce their reliance on fossil fuels. Additionally, passive design strategies such as orienting buildings to maximize natural light and ventilation can further reduce energy consumption.

Construction techniques play a crucial role in achieving net-zero carbon goals as well. By implementing sustainable building practices such as using recycled materials, minimizing waste, and choosing environmentally friendly construction methods, institutions can significantly decrease the environmental impact of their projects. Building materials such as bamboo, recycled steel, and reclaimed wood can not only reduce carbon emissions but also promote a more sustainable supply chain.

Incorporating green building design and construction techniques into projects can also have significant benefits for the occupants of the building. By creating healthier indoor environments with improved air quality, natural light, and thermal comfort, institutions can enhance the well-being and productivity of their occupants. Additionally, sustainable buildings are often more resilient to climate change impacts, such as extreme weather events, which can help protect the safety and security of those inside.

Overall, green building design and construction techniques are essential components of achieving the net-zero carbon concept. By prioritizing sustainability, institutions can reduce their environmental impact, improve the quality of their buildings, and contribute to a more sustainable future. Through a combination of energy-efficient technologies, sustainable materials, and environmentally responsible practices, institutions can play a significant role in decarbonizing the future and creating a more resilient and sustainable built environment.

Advancements in Net-Zero Carbon Construction Materials

In recent years, there have been significant advancements in the development of net-zero carbon construction materials. These materials are designed to minimize greenhouse gas emissions throughout their lifecycle, from production to disposal. By utilizing sustainable materials such as recycled steel, bamboo, and hempcrete, builders can drastically reduce the carbon footprint of their projects. Additionally, innovations in renewable energy sources for construction, such as solar panels and wind turbines, are being integrated into building designs to further reduce carbon emissions.

One key advancement in net-zero carbon construction materials is the development of carbon-negative materials. These materials actively remove carbon dioxide from the atmosphere, helping to offset the emissions generated during the construction process. For example, bio-based materials like timber and straw bales not only have a lower carbon footprint than traditional building materials but also sequester carbon as they grow. By incorporating these materials into construction projects, builders can create buildings that are not only carbon-neutral but actually have a net-negative impact on the environment.

Another important development in net-zero carbon construction materials is the use of advanced insulation and energy-efficient design techniques. By improving the thermal performance of buildings, builders can reduce the energy required for heating and cooling, thereby lowering overall carbon emissions. Materials such as aerogel insulation and triple-glazed windows are being used to create highly efficient building envelopes that minimize energy loss. Additionally, passive design strategies, such as orienting buildings to maximize natural light and ventilation, are being employed to further reduce energy consumption.

Furthermore, the incorporation of smart technologies into building design is revolutionizing the construction industry's approach to achieving net-zero carbon goals. Building automation systems, energy monitoring devices, and advanced HVAC systems are being used to optimize energy use and reduce waste. By integrating these technologies into construction projects, builders can ensure that buildings operate at peak efficiency, minimizing their carbon footprint over time. Additionally, the use of digital tools such as Building Information Modeling (BIM) is enabling architects and engineers to design more sustainable buildings from the outset.

In conclusion, the advancements in net-zero carbon construction materials are paving the way for a more sustainable and environmentally friendly built environment. By utilizing innovative materials, energy-efficient design techniques, and smart technologies, builders can reduce the carbon footprint of their projects and contribute to the global effort to combat climate change. Institutions in all fields and interested people from every specialty have a crucial role to play in adopting these advancements and pushing the boundaries of sustainable construction practices. By working together, we can create a future where net-zero carbon buildings are the norm, rather than the exception.

Chapter 5: Net-Zero Carbon in Energy Production

Transitioning to Renewable Energy Sources

Transitioning to renewable energy sources is crucial in achieving net-zero carbon emissions and combating climate change. Renewable energy sources such as solar, wind, hydroelectric, and geothermal power are abundant, sustainable, and have minimal environmental impact compared to fossil fuels. Institutions in all fields must prioritize transitioning to renewable energy sources to reduce their carbon footprint and contribute to a more sustainable future.

In the transportation sector, transitioning to electric vehicles powered by renewable energy is essential in achieving net-zero carbon emissions. Electric vehicles produce zero tailpipe emissions and can be charged using renewable energy sources, reducing the carbon footprint of transportation. Institutions must invest in electric vehicle infrastructure and promote the adoption of electric vehicles to reduce greenhouse gas emissions from the transportation sector.

In agriculture, transitioning to sustainable farming practices and utilizing renewable energy sources can help reduce carbon emissions. Implementing practices such as organic farming, crop rotation, and agroforestry can sequester carbon in the soil and reduce the carbon footprint of agriculture. Additionally, utilizing renewable energy sources such as solar power for irrigation and farm operations can further reduce emissions in the agricultural sector.

In the construction industry, transitioning to net-zero carbon buildings through energy-efficient design and renewable energy sources is essential. Building designs that prioritize energy efficiency, use sustainable materials, and incorporate renewable energy technologies such as solar panels and geothermal heating can significantly reduce carbon emissions from the construction sector. Institutions must prioritize sustainable building practices and invest in green building technologies to achieve net-zero carbon emissions in the construction industry.

In energy production, transitioning to renewable energy sources such as solar, wind, and hydroelectric power is crucial in reducing carbon emissions. Investing in renewable energy infrastructure and phasing out fossil fuel power plants can help decarbonize the energy sector and transition to a cleaner, more sustainable energy system. Institutions must prioritize renewable energy investments and policies to accelerate the transition to net-zero carbon energy production.

Innovations in Energy Storage Technologies

Innovations in energy storage technologies play a crucial role in achieving the goal of net-zero carbon emissions. As institutions in all fields and interested individuals from every specialty strive towards decarbonizing the future, it is essential to stay informed about the latest advancements in energy storage. These innovations not only help in reducing carbon emissions but also contribute to a more sustainable and efficient energy system.

One of the most significant innovations in energy storage technologies is the development of advanced batteries. These batteries, such as lithium-ion batteries, are becoming increasingly popular for storing renewable energy generated from sources like solar and wind. They have higher energy densities, longer lifespans, and faster charging capabilities, making them ideal for grid-scale energy storage and electric vehicles. Additionally, research is ongoing to improve the performance and sustainability of these batteries, with promising results on the horizon.

Another promising innovation in energy storage is the use of hydrogen as a clean energy carrier. Hydrogen can be produced through electrolysis using renewable electricity and stored for later use in fuel cells to generate electricity. This technology is particularly useful for sectors like heavy-duty transportation and industrial processes that are difficult to electrify directly. As advancements continue to be made in hydrogen storage and infrastructure, it is expected to play a significant role in decarbonizing these hard-to-abate sectors.

Furthermore, thermal energy storage technologies are being developed to store excess heat generated from renewable sources like concentrated solar power plants. This stored heat can be used to generate electricity during periods of low renewable energy generation or high demand, improving the overall efficiency and reliability of renewable energy systems. Innovations in thermal energy storage are crucial for integrating more renewables into the grid and reducing the reliance on fossil fuels for energy generation.

In conclusion, staying informed about innovations in energy storage technologies is essential for institutions in all fields and interested individuals from every specialty. These advancements are key to achieving the goal of net-zero carbon emissions and transitioning to a more sustainable energy system. By investing in and adopting these technologies, we can pave the way for a cleaner, greener future for generations to come.

Policy and Regulatory Frameworks for Net-Zero Carbon Energy Production

Policy and regulatory frameworks play a crucial role in achieving net-zero carbon energy production. In order to effectively transition to a sustainable energy system, it is essential for institutions in all fields and interested individuals from every specialty to understand the importance of implementing policies that support the development of clean energy technologies and the reduction of greenhouse gas emissions. By creating a supportive regulatory environment, governments can incentivize the adoption of renewable energy sources and promote energy efficiency measures that will help to reduce carbon emissions in the long term.

One key aspect of policy and regulatory frameworks for net-zero carbon energy production is the establishment of clear targets and timelines for transitioning to a low-carbon energy system. By setting specific goals for reducing carbon emissions and increasing the share of renewable energy in the energy mix, governments can provide a clear roadmap for industry stakeholders and investors to follow. Additionally, regulatory frameworks can help to ensure that energy producers adhere to strict emission standards and implement measures to reduce their carbon footprint, thereby accelerating the transition to a more sustainable energy system.

Another important consideration in policy and regulatory frameworks for net-zero carbon energy production is the need to promote innovation and investment in clean energy technologies. By providing financial incentives and support for research and development in areas such as renewable energy, energy storage, and carbon capture technologies, governments can help to drive the transition to a low-carbon energy system. Additionally, policies that encourage the deployment of clean energy technologies, such as feed-in tariffs and tax incentives, can help to create a more favorable market environment for renewable energy producers and accelerate the adoption of clean energy solutions.

Furthermore, policy and regulatory frameworks for net-zero carbon energy production should also address the need for a just transition for workers in the fossil fuel industry. As we shift towards a low-carbon energy system, it is important to ensure that workers in traditional energy sectors are not left behind. By implementing policies that support retraining and job creation in clean energy industries, governments can help to ensure a smooth and equitable transition for workers in the fossil fuel sector. Additionally, policies that support the development of sustainable energy communities and promote energy democracy can help to empower communities to take control of their energy future and benefit from the transition to a low-carbon energy system.

In conclusion, policy and regulatory frameworks are essential for achieving net-zero carbon energy production and transitioning to a sustainable energy system. By setting clear targets, promoting innovation, and supporting a just transition for workers, governments can create a supportive environment for the development of clean energy technologies and the reduction of carbon emissions. Institutions in all fields and interested individuals from every specialty have a crucial role to play in advocating for strong policies that will help to accelerate the transition to a low-carbon energy system and create a more sustainable future for all.

Chapter 6: Net-Zero Carbon in Waste Management

Challenges of Waste Management in Achieving Net-Zero Carbon

Waste management plays a crucial role in the journey towards achieving net-zero carbon emissions. However, it presents several challenges that must be addressed in order to effectively reduce the carbon footprint of our waste disposal processes. One major challenge is the lack of proper infrastructure and resources for sustainable waste management practices. Many regions still rely heavily on landfills and incineration, which contribute significantly to greenhouse gas emissions. In order to transition to a net-zero carbon waste management system, investments in recycling facilities, composting plants, and waste-to-energy technologies are essential.

Another challenge in waste management is the issue of contamination and improper sorting of waste streams. Contaminated waste not only hinders recycling efforts but also leads to increased emissions during disposal. Education and awareness campaigns are needed to help individuals and businesses understand the importance of proper waste sorting and disposal practices. Additionally, implementing strict regulations and enforcement mechanisms can help ensure compliance with waste management guidelines and reduce contamination levels.

The concept of a circular economy, where resources are reused, recycled, and repurposed to minimize waste generation, is key to achieving net-zero carbon in waste management. However, the transition to a circular economy requires significant changes in consumer behavior, product design, and supply chain management. Collaboration between government, industry, and the public is essential to drive the adoption of circular economy principles and create a sustainable waste management system that minimizes carbon emissions.

Technological advancements also play a crucial role in addressing the challenges of waste management in achieving net-zero carbon. Innovations such as advanced recycling technologies, waste sorting robots, and digital waste tracking systems can help optimize waste collection, processing, and disposal processes. Investing in research and development of these technologies is essential to improve the efficiency and sustainability of waste management practices.

In conclusion, waste management presents several challenges in achieving net-zero carbon emissions, but with the right strategies and investments, it is possible to create a sustainable waste management system that minimizes carbon footprint. By investing in infrastructure, education, circular economy principles, and technological innovations, institutions in all fields can play a significant role in transitioning towards a net-zero carbon future. It is imperative that stakeholders from every specialty come together to collaborate and drive positive change in waste management practices for a more sustainable and carbon-neutral future.

Strategies for Reducing and Recycling Waste

Institutions in all fields and interested people from every specialty are increasingly recognizing the importance of reducing and recycling waste as part of the overall strategy to achieve net-zero carbon emissions. By implementing effective waste management practices, organizations can not only minimize their environmental impact but also save costs and resources in the long run. In this subchapter, we will explore some key strategies for reducing and recycling waste that can be implemented across various sectors.

One of the most effective strategies for reducing waste is to prioritize waste prevention at the source. This involves identifying opportunities to reduce waste generation through product redesign, process optimization, and the use of more sustainable materials. By minimizing waste generation in the first place, organizations can significantly reduce their environmental footprint and decrease the need for waste disposal and recycling.

In addition to waste prevention, recycling plays a crucial role in achieving net-zero carbon emissions. By implementing effective recycling programs, organizations can divert materials from landfills and incinerators, reduce the demand for virgin resources, and lower greenhouse gas emissions associated with the production of new materials. Recycling also helps to create a circular economy where materials are reused and recycled indefinitely, minimizing the need for resource extraction and reducing waste generation.

Furthermore, organizations can engage in composting organic waste as a sustainable alternative to traditional waste disposal methods. By composting organic waste, organizations can reduce methane emissions from landfills, improve soil health, and create valuable compost that can be used to enrich soil and support sustainable agriculture practices. Composting is a cost-effective and environmentally friendly way to manage organic waste and reduce the overall carbon footprint of an organization.

Lastly, collaboration and partnerships with waste management companies, recycling facilities, and other stakeholders are essential for implementing effective waste reduction and recycling strategies. By working together, organizations can leverage each other's expertise, resources, and networks to develop innovative solutions, share best practices, and drive collective action towards achieving net-zero carbon emissions. By adopting a holistic and collaborative approach to waste management, institutions in all fields can play a significant role in building a more sustainable and resilient future for all.

Waste-to-Energy Solutions for Net-Zero Carbon Goals

In our quest to achieve net-zero carbon goals, waste-to-energy solutions play a crucial role in reducing greenhouse gas emissions and transitioning to a more sustainable future. By converting waste materials into energy, we can not only reduce the amount of waste sent to landfills but also generate clean energy that can help power our communities. Waste-to-energy solutions offer a practical and efficient way to tackle the dual challenges of waste management and carbon emissions reduction.

One of the key benefits of waste-to-energy solutions is their ability to divert organic waste from landfills, where it would otherwise decompose and release methane, a potent greenhouse gas. By capturing methane emissions from organic waste and converting it into energy, we can significantly reduce our carbon footprint and mitigate the impact of waste on the environment. This process not only helps to reduce greenhouse gas emissions but also produces renewable energy that can contribute to our net-zero carbon goals.

Furthermore, waste-to-energy solutions can help to address the growing energy demands of our society while simultaneously reducing our reliance on fossil fuels. By harnessing the energy potential of waste materials, we can create a sustainable source of power that is both environmentally friendly and cost-effective. This can help to diversify our energy sources and move towards a more resilient and sustainable energy system that supports our net-zero carbon objectives.

In addition to reducing greenhouse gas emissions and generating clean energy, waste-to-energy solutions can also help to create new economic opportunities and jobs in the green energy sector. By investing in waste-to-energy technologies and infrastructure, we can stimulate innovation, create new markets, and support the growth of a green economy that is focused on sustainability and climate action. This can help to drive economic growth while also advancing our net-zero carbon goals in a way that benefits both people and the planet.

Overall, waste-to-energy solutions represent a powerful tool in our efforts to achieve net-zero carbon goals and create a more sustainable future. By harnessing the energy potential of waste materials, we can reduce greenhouse gas emissions, generate clean energy, and create new economic opportunities that support our transition to a low-carbon economy. Institutions in all fields and interested individuals from every specialty can play a crucial role in advancing waste-to-energy solutions and driving progress towards a net-zero carbon future.

Chapter 7: Net-Zero Carbon in Urban Planning

Sustainable Urban Development Practices

Sustainable urban development practices play a crucial role in achieving net-zero carbon emissions in the built environment. As institutions in all fields and interested individuals from various specialties are increasingly focused on decarbonizing the future, understanding the key principles of sustainable urban development is essential. By integrating sustainable practices into urban planning, construction, transportation, and waste management, cities can significantly reduce their carbon footprint and contribute to a more sustainable future.

One of the key aspects of sustainable urban development is promoting sustainable transportation systems. By encouraging the use of public transportation, cycling, and walking, cities can reduce greenhouse gas emissions from vehicles and improve air quality. Implementing policies that prioritize pedestrian-friendly infrastructure and efficient public transportation networks can help cities move towards net-zero carbon emissions in the transportation sector.

In addition to transportation, sustainable urban development practices also encompass sustainable construction techniques. By utilizing energy-efficient building materials, incorporating renewable energy sources, and designing buildings with a focus on energy efficiency, cities can reduce the carbon footprint of new construction projects. Retrofitting existing buildings to improve energy efficiency and implementing green building certifications can also contribute to achieving net-zero carbon emissions in the construction industry.

Another important aspect of sustainable urban development is waste management. By implementing recycling programs, composting initiatives, and reducing waste generation through sustainable practices, cities can minimize the amount of waste sent to landfills and reduce methane emissions. Investing in waste-to-energy facilities and promoting circular economy principles can further support efforts to achieve net-zero carbon emissions in waste management.

Overall, sustainable urban development practices are essential for achieving net-zero carbon emissions in cities. By integrating sustainable transportation systems, energy-efficient construction techniques, and innovative waste management strategies, cities can reduce their carbon footprint and create more livable, resilient, and sustainable urban environments. As institutions in all fields and interested individuals from every specialty continue to prioritize decarbonizing the future, sustainable urban development will play a critical role in shaping a more sustainable and low-carbon future.

Green Infrastructure for Net-Zero Carbon Cities

Green infrastructure plays a crucial role in the transition towards net-zero carbon cities. By incorporating natural elements such as green roofs, permeable pavements, and urban green spaces, cities can mitigate the effects of climate change, reduce energy consumption, and improve overall livability. These green infrastructure solutions not only help to sequester carbon dioxide but also provide numerous co-benefits such as improved air quality, reduced urban heat island effect, and enhanced biodiversity.

In the context of transportation, net-zero carbon cities prioritize sustainable modes of transport such as walking, cycling, and public transit. By investing in infrastructure for electric vehicles and promoting car-sharing schemes, cities can significantly reduce their carbon footprint from transportation. Additionally, integrating green spaces and pedestrian-friendly infrastructure into urban planning can further encourage active transportation and reduce reliance on fossil fuel-powered vehicles.

In agriculture, net-zero carbon cities promote sustainable farming practices such as organic agriculture, agroforestry, and regenerative farming. By reducing reliance on synthetic fertilizers and pesticides, cities can lower their greenhouse gas emissions and improve soil health. Additionally, supporting local food systems and promoting plant-rich diets can further reduce the carbon footprint of food production and distribution.

In the construction sector, net-zero carbon cities prioritize energy-efficient building design, materials, and construction techniques. By implementing green building standards such as LEED and Passive House, cities can reduce the energy consumption and emissions associated with buildings. Additionally, incorporating renewable energy sources such as solar panels and geothermal heating can further lower the carbon footprint of the built environment.

Overall, achieving net-zero carbon cities requires a holistic approach that addresses various sectors including energy production, waste management, urban planning, manufacturing, forestry, water management, and consumer goods and services. By integrating green infrastructure solutions across these sectors, cities can not only reduce their greenhouse gas emissions but also create more resilient, sustainable, and livable urban environments for current and future generations.

Community Engagement in Achieving Net-Zero Carbon Urban Environments

Community engagement plays a crucial role in achieving net-zero carbon urban environments. Institutions in all fields and interested individuals from every specialty must come together to work towards this common goal. By educating and involving local communities in the transition to net-zero carbon, we can create sustainable practices that benefit both the environment and society as a whole.

One key aspect of community engagement in achieving net-zero carbon urban environments is raising awareness about the concept itself. Many people may not fully understand what net-zero carbon means or how it can be achieved. By providing education and resources to community members, we can empower them to make informed decisions and act towards reducing carbon emissions in their daily lives.

In the realm of transportation, community engagement is essential for promoting sustainable modes of travel such as walking, cycling, and public transportation. By working with local governments and transportation agencies, communities can advocate for the expansion of bike lanes, pedestrian-friendly infrastructure, and efficient public transportation systems. Through collective action, we can reduce the carbon footprint of our transportation systems and create more livable, healthy urban environments.

In agriculture, community engagement can help promote regenerative farming practices that sequester carbon in the soil and reduce greenhouse gas emissions. By supporting local farmers who adopt sustainable agriculture techniques, communities can not only reduce their carbon footprint but also promote food security and resilience in the face of climate change. Through community-supported agriculture programs and farmers markets, we can strengthen the connection between urban and rural communities and build a more sustainable food system.

In construction, community engagement is essential for promoting energy-efficient building practices and sustainable design principles. By involving local residents in the planning and development of green buildings, communities can create living spaces that are not only environmentally friendly but also affordable and comfortable. Through initiatives such as green building certifications and community-led sustainability projects, we can transform the built environment and pave the way for net-zero carbon urban development.

Chapter 8: Net-Zero Carbon in Manufacturing

Carbon Emissions in the Manufacturing Sector

Carbon emissions in the manufacturing sector play a significant role in contributing to global greenhouse gas emissions. As institutions in all fields and interested people from every specialty, it is crucial to understand the impact of manufacturing activities on the environment and explore ways to reduce carbon emissions to achieve a net-zero carbon future.

Manufacturing processes involve the use of fossil fuels, such as coal, oil, and natural gas, which release carbon dioxide and other greenhouse gases into the atmosphere. These emissions not only contribute to climate change but also have negative effects on air quality and human health. It is imperative for the manufacturing sector to adopt cleaner and more sustainable practices to reduce its carbon footprint.

One way to reduce carbon emissions in the manufacturing sector is to transition to renewable energy sources, such as solar, wind, and hydropower. By using clean energy sources to power manufacturing operations, carbon emissions can be significantly reduced, leading to a more sustainable and environmentally friendly manufacturing process. Additionally, implementing energy-efficient technologies and practices can further help in lowering carbon emissions in the sector.

Another key strategy to decarbonize the manufacturing sector is to improve resource efficiency and promote circular economy principles. By reducing waste generation, reusing materials, and recycling resources, manufacturers can minimize their environmental impact and decrease their carbon footprint. Implementing sustainable supply chain practices and using eco-friendly materials can also contribute to reducing carbon emissions in the manufacturing sector.

Furthermore, investing in research and development to innovate new technologies and processes that are more energy-efficient and environmentally friendly can help in achieving net-zero carbon emissions in the manufacturing sector. Collaborating with other industries, governments, and organizations to share best practices and knowledge can also accelerate the transition to a low-carbon economy. By working together towards a common goal of decarbonization, we can create a more sustainable future for generations to come.

Implementing Sustainable Practices in Manufacturing Processes

In order to achieve a net-zero carbon future, it is imperative for institutions in all fields and interested individuals from every specialty to implement sustainable practices in manufacturing processes. Manufacturing is a significant contributor to greenhouse gas emissions, making it crucial for industries to adopt environmentally friendly practices in their operations. By reducing carbon emissions in manufacturing processes, we can make significant progress towards achieving a net-zero carbon future.

One key aspect of implementing sustainable practices in manufacturing processes is to prioritize energy efficiency. By investing in energy-efficient technologies and equipment, manufacturers can reduce their carbon footprint and lower their energy consumption. This not only helps in reducing greenhouse gas emissions but also results in cost savings for the company. Additionally, utilizing renewable energy sources such as solar or wind power can further reduce the environmental impact of manufacturing processes.

Another important step in implementing sustainable practices in manufacturing processes is to optimize resource usage. This includes minimizing waste generation, recycling materials, and reducing water consumption. By implementing a circular economy approach, where materials are reused and recycled to minimize waste, manufacturers can significantly reduce their environmental impact. Additionally, by using sustainable materials and adopting eco-friendly production methods, manufacturers can further reduce their carbon footprint.

Collaboration and partnerships with suppliers and other stakeholders are also crucial in implementing sustainable practices in manufacturing processes. By working together with suppliers to source sustainable materials and reduce emissions throughout the supply chain, manufacturers can make a greater impact in reducing their carbon footprint. It is important for institutions in all fields to prioritize sustainability in their procurement processes and work towards creating a more sustainable and environmentally friendly manufacturing industry.

Overall, implementing sustainable practices in manufacturing processes is essential for achieving a net-zero carbon future. By prioritizing energy efficiency, optimizing resource usage, and collaborating with suppliers and stakeholders, manufacturers can make significant strides towards reducing their carbon footprint. It is imperative for institutions in all fields and interested individuals from every specialty to work together towards creating a more sustainable and environmentally friendly manufacturing industry.

Circular Economy Approaches for Achieving Net-Zero Carbon in Manufacturing

Circular economy approaches are gaining traction as a key strategy for achieving net-zero carbon emissions in the manufacturing sector. By transitioning from a linear "take-make-dispose" model to one that emphasizes resource efficiency, waste reduction, and recycling, manufacturers can significantly reduce their carbon footprint. This shift requires a fundamental rethinking of how products are designed, produced, and consumed, with a focus on extending product lifecycles and maximizing the value of materials throughout the supply chain.

One key aspect of circular economy approaches in manufacturing is the concept of "closing the loop" on materials, which involves designing products with the end of their life in mind. This means using materials that are easily recyclable or biodegradable, designing for disassembly to facilitate material recovery, and implementing take-back programs to ensure that products are properly recycled or repurposed at the end of their useful life. By keeping materials in circulation and out of landfills, manufacturers can reduce the environmental impact of their operations and minimize the need for virgin resources.

Another important strategy for achieving net-zero carbon in manufacturing is the adoption of renewable energy sources to power production processes. By transitioning to solar, wind, or other clean energy sources, manufacturers can reduce their reliance on fossil fuels and significantly lower their carbon emissions. In addition to reducing greenhouse gas emissions, renewable energy can also help manufacturers reduce their operating costs and increase their resilience to fluctuations in energy prices.

In addition to reducing emissions from their own operations, manufacturers can also contribute to net-zero carbon goals by working with their suppliers and customers to implement circular economy practices throughout the supply chain. This may involve partnering with suppliers to source materials from sustainable and ethical sources, collaborating with customers to design products that are easy to repair and recycle, and engaging with stakeholders to promote sustainable consumption and production practices. By taking a holistic approach to sustainability, manufacturers can not only reduce their own carbon footprint but also drive positive change throughout the entire value chain.

In conclusion, achieving net-zero carbon in manufacturing will require a coordinated effort from all stakeholders, including manufacturers, suppliers, customers, and policymakers. By embracing circular economy approaches, transitioning to renewable energy sources, and collaborating with partners to promote sustainability throughout the supply chain, manufacturers can play a key role in addressing the climate crisis and building a more sustainable future. Through innovation, collaboration, and a commitment to continuous improvement, the manufacturing sector can lead the way towards a net-zero carbon economy.

Chapter 9: Net-Zero Carbon in Forestry and Land Use

The Role of Forests in Carbon Sequestration

Forests play a crucial role in the global effort to combat climate change through carbon sequestration. As trees grow, they absorb carbon dioxide from the atmosphere during photosynthesis and store it in their biomass and soils. This process helps to offset the emissions of greenhouse gases from human activities, making forests a vital natural solution for mitigating climate change. In fact, forests currently absorb around one-third of all human-caused carbon emissions each year, making them a key player in the fight against global warming.

The ability of forests to sequester carbon is particularly important in the context of achieving net-zero carbon emissions. By preserving and expanding forested areas, we can enhance their capacity to capture and store carbon, thereby helping to balance out the remaining emissions that cannot be eliminated through other means. This is why sustainable forest management practices, such as reforestation, afforestation, and reducing deforestation, are essential components of any strategy for achieving net-zero carbon.

Furthermore, forests provide a range of co-benefits beyond carbon sequestration that are crucial for a sustainable future. Forests are essential for biodiversity conservation, watershed protection, and soil health, all of which are critical for maintaining ecosystem services that support human well-being. By prioritizing the preservation and restoration of forests, we can not only mitigate climate change but also safeguard vital ecosystems and promote resilience in the face of environmental challenges.

In order to maximize the potential of forests for carbon sequestration, it is important to address the drivers of deforestation and degradation. This includes tackling issues such as illegal logging, land conversion for agriculture or infrastructure development, and wildfires. By implementing policies and incentives that promote sustainable land use practices and forest conservation, we can ensure that forests continue to play key role in the global carbon cycle.

In conclusion, forests are a valuable ally in the fight against climate change and achieving net-zero carbon emissions. By recognizing the importance of forests for carbon sequestration and implementing measures to protect and enhance their capacity to store carbon, we can make significant progress towards a sustainable future. It is essential that institutions in all fields and interested individuals from every specialty prioritize the conservation and restoration of forests as part of their efforts to decarbonize the future.

Sustainable Land Use Practices for Carbon Reduction

In order to achieve net-zero carbon emissions, it is imperative for institutions in all fields and interested individuals from every specialty to adopt sustainable land use practices. Sustainable land use practices play a crucial role in reducing carbon emissions by promoting carbon sequestration, enhancing biodiversity, and mitigating the impacts of climate change. By implementing sustainable land use practices, we can create a more resilient and sustainable future for generations to come.

One key aspect of sustainable land use practices for carbon reduction is reforestation and afforestation. Trees are natural carbon sinks, absorbing carbon dioxide from the atmosphere and storing it in their biomass. By planting trees and restoring degraded forests, we can increase carbon sequestration and reduce the overall carbon footprint of land use practices. Additionally, reforestation and afforestation can help to enhance biodiversity, improve soil health, and provide valuable ecosystem services.

Another important aspect of sustainable land use practices for carbon reduction is sustainable agriculture. Conventional agriculture practices, such as monocropping and excessive tillage, can contribute to carbon emissions through soil degradation and deforestation. By adopting sustainable agriculture practices, such as agroforestry, cover cropping, and conservation tillage, we can reduce carbon emissions, improve soil health, and increase resilience to climate change. Sustainable agriculture practices also have the potential to sequester carbon in the soil, further reducing the carbon footprint of land use practices.

Urban planning is another key area where sustainable land use practices can play a significant role in reducing carbon emissions. By designing and building sustainable, compact, and walkable cities, we can reduce the need for car travel, lower energy consumption, and decrease carbon emissions. Sustainable urban planning practices such as mixed land use development, green infrastructure, and public transportation can help to create more sustainable and livable communities while reducing the carbon footprint of urban areas.

In conclusion, sustainable land use practices are essential for achieving net-zero carbon emissions and mitigating the impacts of climate change. By implementing sustainable land use practices such as reforestation, sustainable agriculture, and sustainable urban planning, institutions in all fields and interested individuals from every specialty can contribute to a more sustainable and resilient future. It is imperative that we work together to adopt sustainable land use practices and reduce our carbon footprint for the betterment of the planet and future generations.

Forest Management Strategies for Achieving Net-Zero Carbon Goals

Forest management plays a crucial role in achieving net-zero carbon goals, as forests are essential for sequestering carbon dioxide from the atmosphere. To effectively manage forests for carbon sequestration, it is important to adopt sustainable forestry practices that promote the growth and health of trees. This includes practices such as selective logging, reforestation, and agroforestry, which can help increase the carbon storage capacity of forests.

One key strategy for achieving net-zero carbon goals through forest management is the protection and preservation of old-growth forests. Old-growth forests are valuable carbon sinks, as they contain large amounts of carbon stored in their mature trees and soil. By conserving these forests and preventing deforestation, we can maintain their carbon storage capacity and prevent the release of stored carbon into the atmosphere.

Another important aspect of forest management for achieving net-zero carbon goals is the implementation of sustainable harvesting practices. Sustainable forestry practices such as selective logging and tree planting can help maintain the health and productivity of forests while also sequestering carbon dioxide. By carefully managing forest resources and ensuring that trees are harvested in a sustainable manner, we can continue to benefit from the carbon sequestration potential of forests.

In addition to sustainable forestry practices, it is also important to consider the role of forests in providing ecosystem services that support climate mitigation efforts. Forests play a crucial role in regulating the climate by absorbing carbon dioxide and releasing oxygen through photosynthesis. By protecting and restoring forest ecosystems, we can enhance their ability to sequester carbon and contribute to global efforts to combat climate change.

Overall, effective forest management strategies are essential for achieving net-zero carbon goals and mitigating the impacts of climate change. By adopting sustainable forestry practices, protecting old-growth forests, and harnessing the carbon sequestration potential of forests, we can make significant progress towards carbon-neutral future. It is imperative that institutions in all fields and interested individuals from every specialty prioritize forest management as a key component of their efforts to achieve net-zero carbon emissions.

Chapter 10: Net-Zero Carbon in Water Management

Impact of Water Management on Carbon Emissions

Water management plays a crucial role in the overall effort to reduce carbon emissions and achieve a net-zero carbon future. The impact of water management on carbon emissions is significant, as water-related activities can either contribute to or mitigate greenhouse gas emissions. By understanding and implementing sustainable water management practices, institutions in all fields can make a positive impact on the environment and work towards achieving net-zero carbon goals.

One key aspect of water management that affects carbon emissions is the energy required for water treatment and distribution. The process of treating and distributing water consumes a considerable amount of energy, which often comes from fossil fuels. By optimizing water treatment processes, reducing leaks in distribution systems, and investing in energy-efficient technologies, institutions can decrease the carbon footprint associated with water management.

Additionally, water management practices such as wastewater treatment and desalination can also have a significant impact on carbon emissions. Wastewater treatment plants emit methane, a potent greenhouse gas, during the treatment process. By implementing anaerobic digestion and other technologies to capture and utilize methane, institutions can reduce the carbon footprint of wastewater treatment. Similarly, desalination processes can be energy-intensive, but by incorporating renewable energy sources and improving efficiency, institutions can minimize the carbon emissions associated with desalination.

Furthermore, sustainable water management practices can help institutions adapt to and mitigate the effects of climate change, which is essential for achieving net-zero carbon goals. As climate change leads to more frequent and severe droughts, floods, and other water-related challenges, it is crucial for institutions to implement water management strategies that are resilient, resource-efficient, and environmentally sustainable. By investing in green infrastructure, water reuse and recycling, and other innovative solutions, institutions can not only reduce their carbon emissions but also enhance their overall resilience to climate change.

In conclusion, the impact of water management on carbon emissions cannot be understated. By prioritizing sustainable water management practices, institutions in all fields can play a significant role in reducing their carbon footprint and working towards a net-zero carbon future. Through efficient water treatment and distribution, methane capture in wastewater treatment, energy-efficient desalination, and climate-resilient water management strategies, institutions can make a positive impact on the environment and contribute to a more sustainable future for generations to come.

Implementing Sustainable Water Practices for Net-Zero Carbon

Implementing sustainable water practices is a crucial aspect of achieving net-zero carbon emissions in various sectors. Water management plays a significant role in reducing carbon footprint and ensuring environmental sustainability. Institutions in all fields must prioritize sustainable water practices to contribute to the overall goal of decarbonizing the future.

One key strategy for implementing sustainable water practices is reducing water consumption through efficient systems and technologies. This includes investing in water-saving fixtures, implementing rainwater harvesting systems, and optimizing irrigation practices in agriculture. By reducing water usage, institutions can also reduce the energy required for water treatment and distribution, leading to lower carbon emissions.

In addition to reducing water consumption, institutions can also focus on enhancing water quality through proper treatment and filtration methods. Implementing sustainable water treatment practices not only ensures clean and safe water for various purposes but also minimizes the environmental impact of water pollution. By prioritizing water quality, institutions can contribute to a healthier ecosystem and reduce the carbon footprint associated with water contamination.

Furthermore, incorporating water conservation practices into urban planning and construction projects is essential for achieving net-zero carbon goals. Green infrastructure, such as permeable pavements and green roofs, can help capture and treat stormwater runoff, reducing the strain on municipal water systems and minimizing pollution. By integrating sustainable water practices into urban development, institutions can create more resilient and environmentally friendly communities.

Overall, implementing sustainable water practices is a critical step towards achieving net-zero carbon emissions. By reducing water consumption, enhancing water quality and integrating water conservation into various sectors, institutions can play significant role in decarbonizing the future. It is imperative for institutions in all fields to prioritize sustainable water management practices to contribute to a more sustainable and carbon-neutral future.

Water Conservation and Reuse Strategies for a Net-Zero Carbon Future

Water conservation and reuse strategies are critical components in achieving a net-zero carbon future. As institutions in all fields and interested individuals from every specialty work towards decarbonizing the future, it is essential to understand the importance of sustainable water management practices. By reducing water consumption and implementing innovative water reuse technologies, organizations can significantly decrease their carbon footprint and contribute to a more sustainable future.

One key strategy for water conservation is the implementation of water-efficient technologies and practices. This includes using low-flow fixtures, implementing water recycling systems, and optimizing water use in agricultural and industrial processes. By reducing water waste and improving water efficiency, institutions can lower their overall carbon emissions and minimize their impact on the environment. Additionally, investing in water-saving technologies can lead to cost savings and improved operational efficiency.

In addition to water conservation, water reuse plays a crucial role in achieving a net-zero carbon future. By treating and reusing wastewater for non-potable purposes such as irrigation, cooling, and industrial processes, organizations can reduce their reliance on freshwater sources and minimize the energy required for water treatment and distribution. Implementing water reuse strategies not only conserves valuable resources but also helps to mitigate the carbon emissions associated with traditional water management practices.

Furthermore, integrating water conservation and reuse strategies into urban planning and infrastructure development is essential for creating sustainable and resilient communities. By incorporating green infrastructure, such as rain gardens, bioswales, and permeable pavement, cities can reduce stormwater runoff, improve water quality, and enhance overall water efficiency. Additionally, promoting water sensitive design practices in buildings and public spaces can help to minimize water consumption and support a more sustainable water management system.

Overall, water conservation and reuse strategies are integral to achieving a net-zero carbon future. By prioritizing sustainable water management practices, institutions in all fields and interested individuals from every specialty can contribute to a more environmentally friendly and resilient future. Through the implementation of water efficient technologies, water reuse systems, and water-sensitive urban planning initiatives, organizations can reduce their carbon footprint, conserve valuable resources, and create a more sustainable world for future generations.

Chapter 11: Net-Zero Carbon in Consumer Goods and Services

Carbon Footprint of Consumer Goods and Services

Consumer goods and services play a significant role in contributing to the overall carbon footprint of individuals and households. From the production and transportation of goods to the energy consumption involved in their use, every aspect of the lifecycle of consumer products has an impact on our environment. Understanding and reducing this carbon footprint is essential in our transition towards achieving net-zero carbon emissions.

When we talk about the carbon footprint of consumer goods and services, we must consider the entire supply chain involved in bringing these products to market. This includes the extraction of raw materials, manufacturing processes, packaging, transportation, and ultimately, the disposal or recycling of the product. Each of these steps contributes to the overall carbon emissions associated with a product, making it crucial for consumers and businesses to consider the environmental impact of their purchasing decisions.

One way to reduce the carbon footprint of consumer goods and services is by choosing products that are produced using sustainable and environmentally friendly practices. This includes opting for products that are made from recycled materials, have a lower energy consumption during production, or are produced locally to reduce transportation emissions. By making conscious choices in our consumption habits, we can significantly reduce the carbon emissions associated with the goods and services we use on a daily basis.

Another important aspect to consider when it comes to the carbon footprint of consumer goods and services is the energy consumption involved in their use. From household appliances to electronic devices, the energy required to power these products contributes to our overall carbon emissions. By choosing energy-efficient products and reducing our overall energy consumption, we can lower the carbon footprint associated with our consumer goods and services.

In conclusion, understanding and reducing the carbon footprint of consumer goods and services is essential in our efforts to achieve net-zero carbon emissions. By considering the entire lifecycle of products, choosing sustainable and environmentally friendly options, and reducing energy consumption, we can make a significant impact on our environment. It is crucial for institutions in all fields and interested individuals to be mindful of their consumption habits and work towards a more sustainable future for all.

Sustainable Consumption Practices for Net-Zero Carbon

In order to achieve a net-zero carbon future, sustainable consumption practices are paramount. Institutions in all fields and interested individuals from every specialty must understand the importance of reducing their carbon footprint through conscious consumption habits. By making informed choices about the products we use and the resources we consume, we can contribute significantly to the global effort of decarbonizing our future.

One key aspect of sustainable consumption practices for net-zero carbon is in transportation. From opting for electric vehicles to utilizing public transportation and carpooling, there are various ways in which institutions and individuals can reduce their carbon emissions in the transportation sector. By prioritizing sustainable modes of transportation, we can minimize our impact on the environment and work towards a net-zero carbon future.

Another crucial area where sustainable consumption practices can make a significant difference is in agriculture. By supporting regenerative farming practices, reducing food waste, and choosing locally sourced and organic products, institutions and individuals can lower their carbon footprint in the agricultural sector. By promoting sustainable agriculture, we can not only reduce emissions but also support biodiversity and soil health.

In the construction industry, sustainable consumption practices play a vital role in achieving net-zero carbon goals. By using eco-friendly building materials, designing energy-efficient structures, and incorporating renewable energy systems, institutions can minimize the carbon footprint of their construction projects. Sustainable building practices not only help reduce emissions but also create healthier and more resilient buildings for the future.

In energy production, waste management, urban planning, manufacturing, forestry and land use, water management, and consumer goods and services, there are countless opportunities for institutions and individuals to adopt sustainable consumption practices for net-zero carbon. By being mindful of the environmental impact of our choices and taking proactive steps towards sustainability, we can all contribute to a greener, cleaner, and more sustainable future for generations to come.

Promoting Eco-Friendly Choices for a Net-Zero Carbon Lifestyle

As we strive towards a more sustainable future, promoting eco-friendly choices is crucial in achieving a net-zero carbon lifestyle. Institutions in all fields and interested individuals from every specialty play a significant role in making informed decisions that prioritize the health of our planet. By understanding the net-zero carbon concept and how it can be achieved, we can collectively work towards a greener and more sustainable future.

One key area where eco-friendly choices can have a significant impact is in transportation. By promoting the use of electric vehicles, public transportation, and active modes of transportation such as walking and cycling, we can reduce our carbon footprint and decrease greenhouse gas emissions. Institutions can support and incentivize the adoption of sustainable transportation options to help reduce the environmental impact of commuting and travel.

Another important aspect of promoting eco-friendly choices is in agriculture. By supporting regenerative farming practices, organic farming methods, and reducing food waste, institutions can contribute to a more sustainable food system. By prioritizing local and seasonal produce, reducing meat consumption, and supporting sustainable farming practices, we can help reduce the carbon footprint of our food supply chain.

In the construction sector, promoting eco-friendly choices can have a significant impact on reducing carbon emissions. By using sustainable building materials, implementing energy-efficient design principles, and prioritizing renewable energy sources, institutions can help create buildings that are more energy-efficient and environmentally friendly. By investing in green building certifications and sustainable construction practices, we can reduce the carbon footprint of the built environment.

In conclusion, promoting eco-friendly choices for a net-zero carbon lifestyle is essential for creating a more sustainable future. By understanding the net-zero carbon concept and how it can be achieved, institutions in all fields and interested individuals from every specialty can work together to make informed decisions that prioritize the health of our planet. By focusing on sustainable transportation, agriculture, construction, energy production, waste management, urban planning, manufacturing, forestry and land use, water management, and consumer goods and services, we can collectively work towards a greener and more sustainable future.

Conclusion: Moving Towards a Net-Zero Carbon Future

In conclusion, as we move towards a net-zero carbon future, it is imperative that institutions in all fields and interested individuals from every specialty come together to work towards a common goal of reducing our carbon footprint. The concept of net-zero carbon is achievable through a combination of technological advancements, policy changes, and behavioral shifts. By understanding the importance of reducing carbon emissions and implementing sustainable practices, we can create a more environmentally friendly world for future generations.

One key area where we can make significant strides towards achieving net-zero carbon is in transportation. By investing in electric vehicles, improving public transportation systems, and promoting alternative modes of transportation such as biking and walking, we can reduce greenhouse gas emissions and improve air quality in our communities. Additionally, transitioning to renewable energy sources for powering transportation vehicles is essential in achieving a net-zero carbon future.

Another critical area for achieving net-zero carbon is in agriculture. By implementing regenerative farming practices, reducing food waste, and promoting sustainable land management techniques, we can significantly reduce the carbon footprint of the agricultural sector. Additionally, transitioning to plant-based diets and supporting local, organic food systems can further contribute to a more sustainable and carbon-neutral food supply chain.

In the construction industry, transitioning to green building practices, using sustainable materials, and implementing energy-efficient designs can help reduce the carbon emissions associated with building construction and maintenance. By prioritizing energy efficiency, renewable energy sources, and green building certifications, we can create more sustainable and environmentally friendly buildings that contribute to a net-zero carbon future.

Overall, achieving a net-zero carbon future requires a collective effort from all sectors of society. By focusing on reducing carbon emissions in transportation, agriculture, construction, energy production, waste management, urban planning, manufacturing, forestry and land use, water management, and consumer goods and services, we can work towards a more sustainable and environmentally friendly future. It is essential that institutions and individuals alike prioritize sustainability and take proactive steps towards reducing their carbon footprint to create a more sustainable world for future generations.

References:

In order to delve deeper into the concepts and strategies outlined in this book, we recommend the following key references for institutions in all fields and interested individuals from every specialty. These resources provide valuable insights and practical guidance on achieving net-zero carbon emissions in various sectors:

1. "Drawdown: The Most Comprehensive Plan Ever Proposed to Reverse Global Warming" by Paul Hawken - This groundbreaking book offers a comprehensive analysis of the top 100 solutions to reduce greenhouse gas emissions and combat climate change. It serves as a valuable resource for understanding the potential impact of different strategies in decarbonizing the future.

2. "The Carbon-Free City Handbook" by Woodrow Clark and Grant Cooke - This handbook provides a detailed roadmap for cities and urban planners to transition to carbon-neutral future. It offers practical solutions for reducing emissions in transportation, energy production, waste management, and urban planning, making a must-read for those interested in sustainable urban development.

3. "Sustainable Agriculture and Food Systems" by Danielle Nierenberg - This book explores the role of agriculture in achieving net-zero carbon emissions and sustainable food production. It highlights innovative practices and technologies that can help reduce the carbon footprint of the agricultural sector, making it essential reading for those involved in agriculture and food systems.

4. "Green Building and Sustainable Construction" by Michelle Cottrell - This comprehensive guide provides insights into sustainable construction practices that can help reduce carbon emissions in the built environment. It covers topics such as energy-efficient building design, green materials, and renewable energy integration, offering valuable information for construction professionals and policymakers.

5. "Renewable Energy: Power for a Sustainable Future" by Godfrey Boyle - This authoritative text explores the potential of renewable energy sources in decarbonizing the energy sector. It covers a wide range of topics, including solar, wind, hydro, and geothermal energy, making it a valuable resource for those interested in transitioning to a low-carbon energy system.

By consulting these references, institutions and individuals can gain a deeper understanding of the net-zero carbon concept and learn about the strategies and technologies that can help achieve this ambitious goal in various sectors. These resources serve as valuable tools for driving forward the transition to a sustainable and carbon-neutral future.

Acknowledgments

We would like to extend our heartfelt gratitude to the institutions in all fields and interested individuals from every specialty who have contributed their expertise and knowledge to the development of this comprehensive guide to net-zero carbon concepts. Your dedication to sustainability and commitment to reducing carbon emissions have been instrumental in shaping the contents of this book.

In particular, we would like to thank the experts in the fields of transportation, agriculture, construction, energy production, waste management, urban planning, manufacturing, forestry and land use, water management, and consumer goods and services for sharing their insights and best practices for achieving net-zero carbon emissions. Your contributions have provided invaluable insights into the challenges and opportunities in each sector, as well as practical strategies for transitioning to a net-zero carbon future.

We are also grateful to the policymakers, researchers, and industry leaders who have supported our efforts to raise awareness about the importance of decarbonizing our economy and society. Your guidance and input have helped to ensure that this guide is both comprehensive and accessible to a wide range of audiences, from seasoned professionals to students and interested individuals.

Additionally, we would like to express our appreciation to the organizations and initiatives that are actively working towards achieving net-zero carbon goals, whether through innovative technologies, sustainable practices, or advocacy efforts. Your dedication to creating a more sustainable future is inspiring and serves as a model for others to follow.

Finally, we would like to thank our readers for their interest in the net-zero carbon concept and their commitment to making a positive impact on the environment. By working together and sharing our knowledge and expertise, we can create a more sustainable and resilient future for generations to come.

Made in the USA
Columbia, SC
21 August 2024

39832499R00041